The Scented Flower Project Book

Joanna Sheen

Published in 1993 by Merehurst Limited
Ferry House, 51-57 Lacy Road, Putney, London SW15 1PR

ISBN 1-85391-288-3

A catalogue record for this book is available from the British Library.

Managing Editor **Heather Dewhurst**
Edited by **Diana Lodge**
Designed by **Lisa Tai**
Photography by **Debbie Patterson**
Styling assistant **Camilla Bambrough**

Acknowledgements
Merehurst would like to thank the following for loaning props for photography:
Basia Zarzycka, Front shop, Antiquarius, 135 Kings Road, London SW3.

Typesetting by **Litho Link Limited**
Colour separation by **Fotographics Ltd UK - Hong Kong**
Printed in Italy by **New Interlitho S.p.A.**

Contents

Introduction

Flowers, in any shape or form, can be one of the most uplifting sights. A host of golden daffodils or a single snowdrop, a beautiful display of perfectly preserved dried roses and peonies or a tiny bunch of garden flowers picked by a child – any of these can be a wonderful tonic, but the memory that lingers is often the smell, for scents can be powerful reminders of times past and special people in your life.

Adding perfume to a flower arrangement gives it another dimension, and making your own pot pourri can prove a very interesting and relaxing pastime. Lavender and other herbs will always be among my favourite plants, for these have a subtle but lingering perfume.

The projects contained in this book are designed to inspire and persuade you to try your hand at something new. Working with essential oils is fascinating, and whether the arrangement that catches your eye is a fresh display or pot pourri, I hope you will enjoy experimenting with these ideas.

Scented flower basics

Smells or fragrances are very much a matter of personal taste, and what suits one person may not be the choice of another. However, the natural smells of flowers are usually widely acceptable; they are often light and subtle, with a pretty fragrance that can waft through the house if you place the flowers in a spot where you will pass them frequently.

Growing Fragrant Flowers

There are many plants that can be included in a garden to add perfume to a summer's evening or sweet scents to a vase of flowers. The first flower that comes to mind must be the rose. The perfume of a rose is legendary and has been prized for hundreds of years. Sadly, many roses are now bred for their blooms and less importance is given to their scent. There are still, however, many varieties that will give a magnificent perfume, such as the Bourbon rose 'Madame Isaac Pereire', or the *rugosa* variety 'Frau Dagmar Hastrup'. Many other roses have a fragrance, and it is worth seeking out old roses and planting them with a mixture of aromatic herbs such as rue, mint, rosemary and lemon balm to make a stroll in the garden even more pleasurable.

Herbs are another collection of plants that are simple to grow and work very hard for the amount of space they are allocated in the garden. Once you have established a bed of herbs, you will find endless uses for them, both in the kitchen and for decorative and medicinal purposes. A large clump of lavender by the back door may be reminiscent of the old cottage gardens but smells just as wonderful as you go in and out, if your home is a modern house or ground floor apartment.

If you enjoy having flowers in the house, then why not plan your garden with that thought in mind? If you put together several flowering species that bloom at the same time, there may be a noticeable gap when you pick them to fill a vase. Try to plant carefully, so that there are several items with attractive foliage mixed with the star flowering plants; with planning, cutting for the house will leave the garden unspoilt. In this way, you will be able to enjoy the colours and scents of garden flowers indoors, without offending a garden-loving partner.

Drying and Preserving Scents

There are several ways to add perfume to your home; the obvious one is to use fresh flowers and foliage to decorate the house. In these days of central heating, however, fresh arrangements can be very short lived, and dried flowers or pot pourri can give wonderful aromas to all parts of the home.

Although it is now easier to purchase dried flowers and ingredients for pot pourri, nothing compares with the satisfaction of growing your own materials in the garden and drying them. Producing your finished arrangements from seed is very pleasing and reduces the cost considerably.

Air Drying Flowers

The easiest way to dry flowers, seed heads and grasses is to tie them into bunches that are from small to medium in size and secure them with elastic bands. Hang these bunches upside down in a warm and preferably shady area to minimize the natural light that they will receive. The flowers will take from a week to a month to dry, depending upon the variety. You can check whether they are dry by pressing the stem at the base of the flower or seed head; if this is hard, then the flower is ready to use.

Drying Ingredients in the Microwave

Drying plant materials in the microwave for use in pot pourri is quick and can be great fun, as you achieve instant results. This method, however, is not suitable for larger flowers or indeed for materials to be used in arrangements, as the finished shapes are not good enough.

To dry pieces of herbs or flower heads for use in pot pourri, take a couple of sheets of kitchen paper and use this as a base. Lay the sprigs of herb on the paper and place into the microwave. Use medium-to-full heat and cook for between 1½ and 2½ minutes, depending on the size and amount of plant material in the oven. Once the herbs feel dry, remove them from the oven and allow them to cool for five or ten minutes. Experiment with your particular model as times and temperatures vary from oven to oven. Many items can be dried in this way – scented rose petals, for example – but whole flowers will lose their shape and be suitable only for pot pourri.

Another option is to use essential oils to add perfume. These are extracted from plants and contain no chemicals, only the natural oil from the flower, leaf or fruit concerned. Available from chemists and health food stores as well as the sources mentioned at the end of the book, these open up a whole new world of scents, and it can be very absorbing to experiment with new fragrances and combinations.

Herbs are often heavily scented, and their fragrance mingles delightfully with floral smells.

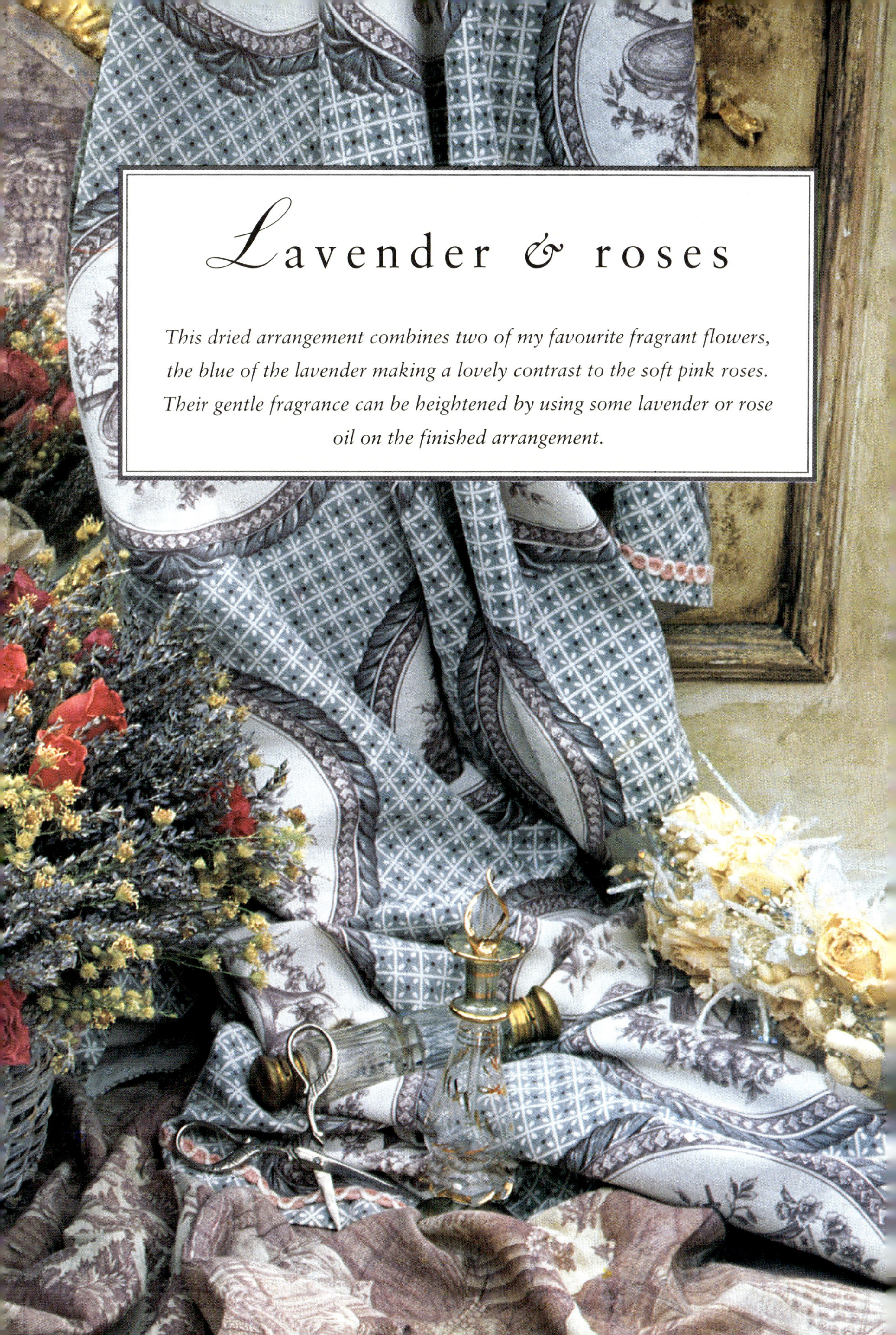

Lavender & roses

This dried arrangement combines two of my favourite fragrant flowers, the blue of the lavender making a lovely contrast to the soft pink roses. Their gentle fragrance can be heightened by using some lavender or rose oil on the finished arrangement.

Lavender & roses

This very special arrangement is simple to make but includes some luxurious ingredients that will make it a basket to be treasured. There are many varieties of lavender; this is an English type – *Lavandula spica* – which is easily grown in the garden. The roses are the commercially-grown varieties, 'Europa' and 'Gerdo', which could be bought fresh and dried at home. I have used four large bunches of lavender and forty roses, twenty of each variety. The other flowers are a bunch of dried asters, which add a dainty touch to the arrangement.

Ingredients

A medium-sized basket with a base approximately 25cm (10in) in diameter

One block of dry foam and one pronged foam attachment

Dried lavender, roses and asters

Four lace-edged handkerchiefs in cream or white

1 *Glue the pronged attachment to the base of the basket and press the foam block on top, trimming the foam to fit. Separate the lavender into bundles of nine or ten stalks and, using all four bunches, fill the basket evenly.*

2 Strip all the leaves from the rose stems; cut them to a suitable length, and then insert them amongst the lavender, one by one. The roses can be spread evenly amongst the lavender or placed in small groups of three or five flowers together. The colour scheme of the basket could easily be altered by changing the varieties of rose.

3 Add some small bunches of the asters to lighten the arrangement. Make sure that they are not longer than the lavender, or they will overshadow this very important ingredient. Finally, tuck the lace-edged handkerchiefs into the basket placing one at each side of the handle.

Flowers for the table

When planning flowers to decorate the table, always be careful to choose lightly-scented flowers rather than something too overpowering, as this can detract from the food! This combination of fruit and flowers would make a talking point for any party.

Flowers for the table

Using fresh lemons and limes adds an exciting novelty to this arrangement. The aromatic herbal greeneries blend together to make a soft greeny-grey foil to the bright yellow of the fruit and flowers. Six apples, two lemons and four limes were used here, but there is an ever-increasing range of exotic fruits now on offer, and you might have fun experimenting with other ingredients, such as star fruit, green tomatoes or small yellow peppers, always aiming for an attractive balance of scent, colour and form.

Ingredients

Fruits (see above)

Seven large pale yellow roses

Herbs – one small bunch of tansy leaves and one of rue ('Jackman's Blue'), and a bunch of dill flowers

Shallow oval serving dish

Quarter block of green florist's foam

1 Put the dill and the roses in a bucket of water until needed to make sure that the flowers do not wilt. Soak the foam in water and then place it in the middle of the serving dish. Cover a diagonal stripe of the foam with foliage – this could be any herbal greenery of a muted greeny grey.

2 Put the fruit into position, making sure you have the same number of each variety at each side of the arrangement.

3 Cut the stems of the dill fairly short – about 4–5cm (1½–2in) – and disperse it among the foliage, keeping the diagonal effect running across the foam block.

4 Finally, insert the roses in the arrangement. As with the dill flowers, the roses will last much longer if they have been given plenty of water before they are used. Possible substitutes for the roses include yellow lilies, pale yellow tulips, or perhaps white roses.

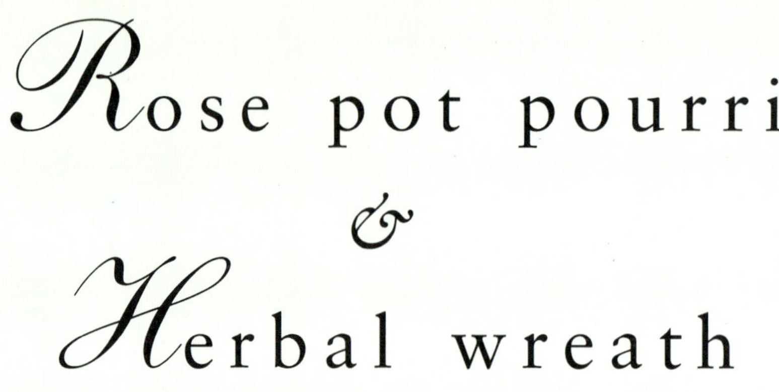

Rose pot pourri & Herbal wreath

Making your own pot pourri creates a mixture that bears no resemblance to any commercial blends, and possesses infinitely prettier colour and fragrance. A fresh herbal wreath is also unlikely to be available commercially.

Rose pot pourri

The colour scheme of this pot pourri is rose pink, creamy white and green, but the basic instructions can be used with any combination of ingredients. Your own pot pourri mixture will be far more interesting than any commercially-produced pot pourri and you can choose your own fragrance or just rely on the natural fragrance of the roses. This blend contains approximately a cupful of each of the following dried ingredients: small red roses, pink roses, small green leaves (box or privet work quite well), pink peony petals and white larkspur. You should choose something spectacular to decorate the top; I have used two small peonies.

Ingredients

Dried flowers and petals (see above)

7g (¼oz) of orris root powder

40–50 drops of perfume oil or essential oil of your choice (here, 25 drops rose oil, 15 lavender oil and 5 clove oil; one teaspoon holds about 60 drops)

Ceramic or glass bowl for mixing

Large polythene bag with tie

1 Prepare your dried materials (see pages 6–7). Measure very roughly one cup of each of the petal and leaf ingredients into a ceramic bowl. You can easily alter the mixture according to what is available in your garden; most combinations will work.

2 Add the oil to the ingredients first, counting the drops, and then add the powdered orris root. Using a metal spoon, stir and fold in the oil and orris root very gently, taking great care not to damage or break up too many of the flowers and other ingredients. If you do not want to add the orris root then it can be omitted, but the strength of the perfume will be weakened and the pot pourri will not smell strongly for very long. The orris root acts as a fixative for the oil and keeps the scent within the mixture for much longer.

3 Empty the bowl into a large plastic bag and tie the neck tightly. Keep it in a cupboard or other dark place for a week or two to enable the fragrances to blend together and mature. Shake or stir the ingredients regularly, to distribute the oils evenly. If you are not happy with the perfume after a week or so, more drops can be added to alter the composition of the fragrance and the mixture can then be returned to the bag for another week or two. Finally, display the pot pourri in an open bowl and decorate the top with some special flowers, such as the air-dried peonies seen here.

Herbal wreath

This wonderful herbal wreath would look stunning in a kitchen and has a secondary use as a source of dried herbs. You can make the wreath with fresh herbs and allow them to dry naturally, or you could dry the herbs in a microwave first and then attach them to the ring. The components of the ring can vary according to the plants that are easily at hand. Herbs are available in supermarkets, greengrocers and many other sources now, so it should not be too difficult to obtain some even if you don't grow them yourself. You will need six fairly large bunches of herbs; I have used parsley, rosemary, bay leaves, mint, lavender and thyme.

Ingredients

Six bunches of herbs (see above)

One vine or willow ring, with a diameter of approximately 25cm (10in)

0.71mm (22 gauge) florists' wires, for bunching

A glue gun and glue

1 *First attach some of the bay leaves – I have used fresh leaves but you could easily use ready dried ones. Then position the rosemary; this dries beautifully on the wreath, so there is no need to dry it beforehand. The stems can either be wired together in bunches or glued on individually.*

2 Continue to build the design around the ring by adding the mint, wired in medium-sized clumps. These can be attached fresh or dried. The lavender is also wired into bunches; I have used dried lavender but either fresh or dried is suitable, providing the lavender is in flower at the time you wish to make the wreath. Try to get an even shape all around the ring, with a reasonably thick covering of ingredients, so that the components like mint and thyme do not look too thin when they dry, leaving gaps in the ring.

3 Add the last two ingredients – the thyme and parsley. I have used both of these fresh as they become a little brittle when dried. Bunch them both thickly to compensate for the extent to which they will shrink as they are drying. Other ingredients could be added according to your taste. If you want to decorate the ring with ribbons, these could be added now, or perhaps you might opt for a raffia bow.

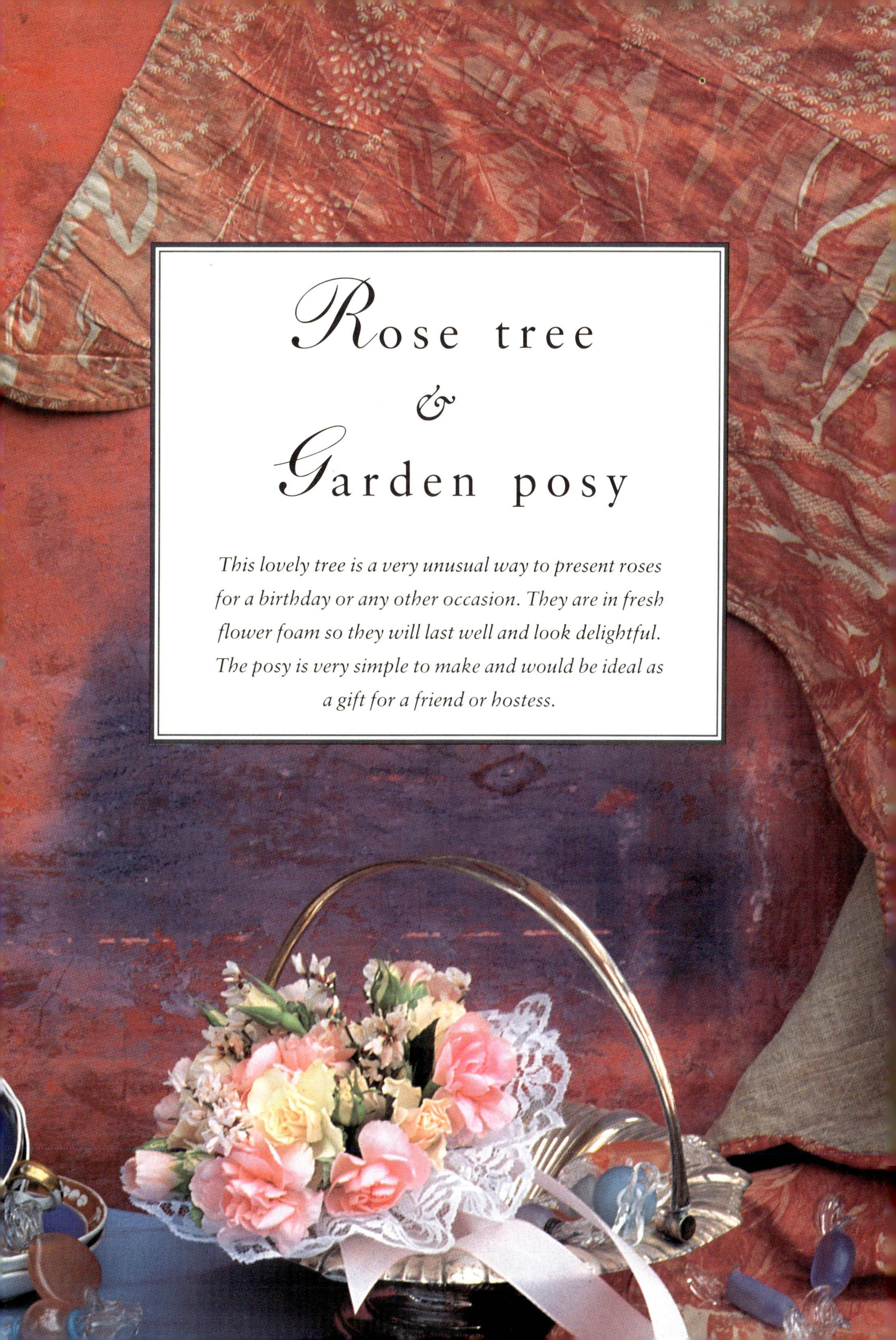

Rose tree & Garden posy

This lovely tree is a very unusual way to present roses for a birthday or any other occasion. They are in fresh flower foam so they will last well and look delightful. The posy is very simple to make and would be ideal as a gift for a friend or hostess.

Rose tree

The clear pink roses are here prettily paired with some unsophisticated feverfew daisies, and the result is a charming tree that would make an unusual gift or treat – perhaps from you to yourself. You will need two dozen spray roses, a bunch of fresh bay, and a large bunch of feverfew. To make the tree base: first, if there is a hole in the terracotta pot, cover it with cardboard; fill the pot up to two-thirds with cement; when the mixture has stiffened a little, insert a stick, approximately 40cm (16in) high, to act as the trunk, and leave to dry for two to three days.

Ingredients

Flowers and leaves (see above)

Tree base in a 12.5cm (5in) terracotta pot

One block of green florist's foam

One green foam ball, 9cm (3½in) in diameter

2m (2yds) of ribbon, 6mm (¼in) wide

0.46mm (26 gauge) florist's wires

***1** Soak the foam, then cut the block to cover the cement; it should lie level with the rim of the pot. Push the ball onto the 'trunk'. Cover the ball and the foam base with bay sprigs. Cut the ribbon in half; form each length into loops, secured with wire, and insert one into the ball, near the trunk, and the other into the base.*

2 Wire small bunches of feverfew, trimming the stems to about 5–7.5cm (2–3in). Place the bunches around the tree and the base, taking care to achieve an even coverage with the daisy-like flowers.

3 Separate the sprays of roses into individual stems, trimming each stem to the same length as the feverfew. Place the roses into the arrangement, again making sure that you have an even coverage, and also making a final check all around to ensure that no foam is visible when you have finished.

Garden posy

A few flowers can quickly be turned into a very attractive gift by presenting them in a pretty posy frill. Providing you keep all the stalks to a similar length, the posy can be put into a vase once it has been received. You will need a small bunch of 'Doris' pinks, three or four sprays of roses, seven scented geranium leaves, and a small bunch of broom.

Ingredients

Flowers and leaves (see above)

A cream or white posy frill, 20cm (8in) in diameter

A reel of rose wire

1m (3ft) of ribbon, 2.5cm (1in) wide, to tone with the colours in the posy

1 First take three pinks and then the scented geranium leaves; bind these together in a bunch, and then bind in some broom. As you add materials, keep the wire in one place on the bunch rather than letting it travel up and down the stalks.

2 Add in the spray roses and keep binding, moderately tightly, in the same position. If you pull too hard on the wire, you will cut the stems, but if the wire is too loose, the posy will fall apart, so aim for a happy medium!

3 Continue to bind in the ingredients: add some more 'Doris' pinks, then look at the shape of the circle and take in extra materials, choosing whatever you consider necessary to keep the shape. Finally, push the posy frill up the stems until you can push no further, and tie the ribbon as tightly as possible around the base of the posy frill, to hold it in position. Tie the ends of the ribbon into a bow.

Chilli kitchen wreath

This bright, cheerful ring, with its unexpected combination of spicy aromas, is designed to decorate a kitchen or family room. It is very easily made, being based on a vine or twig wreath and constructed with a glue gun.

Chilli kitchen wreath

Both the chillis and the cinnamon have natural fragrances of their own, but this can be enhanced by adding a little cinnamon oil or another suitable fragrance to the wreath once it is finished. You will need three or four large hydrangea heads, a bunch of 10 red ('Mercedes') and another of 10 golden/apricot ('Calypso') roses, about 15 slices of apple and 20–30 chillis, a few sticks of cinnamon and a spray of red pepper berries. All the ingredients are dried.

INGREDIENTS

Dried materials (see above)

One willow, vine or twig ring, about 30cm (12in) in diameter

60cm (24in) of tartan or checked ribbon, 5cm (2in) wide

30cm (12in) of matching ribbon, 2.5cm (1in) wide

About 15cm (6in) of 0.71mm (22 gauge) florists' wire

A glue gun and glue

1 Form the wider ribbon into a figure of eight, as shown on page 48; wrap the wire firmly around the middle, making a bow, and knot the narrower ribbon over the wire, making two more streamers. Glue the bow to the base of the ring. Separate the hydrangeas into florets and glue these around the ring.

2 Glue three cinnamon sticks across the bow, attaching them one at a time. Further pieces of cinnamon could be included in the design if you wish. Take the apple slices and attach them in groups of three, placing them around the ring. The apple slices can be produced by slicing a fresh apple and drying the slices in a low oven for three or four hours until dry and leathery.

3 Strip the leaves away from the stems of the roses and trim the stems back until they measure about 2.5–5cm (1–2in). Glue in the rose heads, again in small groups, either keeping the colours separate or mixing them together. Other roses or cheaper flowers could be used to reduce the cost of the project or to change the colour scheme. Finally, glue in the chilli peppers one by one; position them in a fairly random fashion around the ring, including some with the group of items on the bow. Add the spray of pepper berries to the bow.

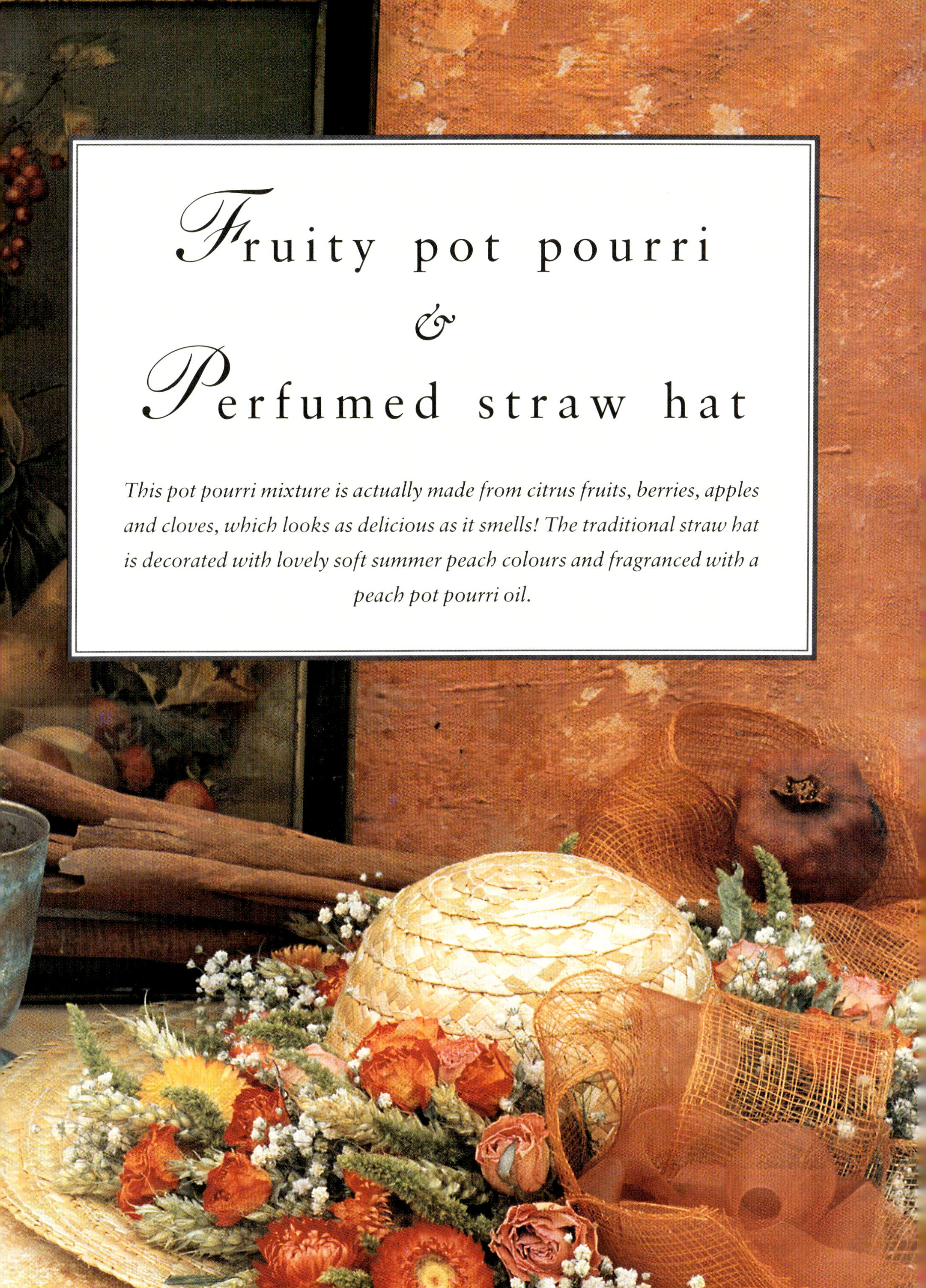

Fruity pot pourri & Perfumed straw hat

This pot pourri mixture is actually made from citrus fruits, berries, apples and cloves, which looks as delicious as it smells! The traditional straw hat is decorated with lovely soft summer peach colours and fragranced with a peach pot pourri oil.

Fruity pot pourri

All the fruit used in this pot pourri is dried in the same way. Slice the fruit fairly thickly; place it on a cake rack in a cool oven, and leave until dry. The apples generally take three to four hours, but the citrus fruit may take longer. The rose hips, pomegranates and apples or oranges studded with cloves were dried over a radiator for about one to two weeks. I have used one of each fruit sliced, three tablespoons of orange peel and three of dried chillies, six to eight broken cinnamon sticks, three cups of small red roses or petals and one of rose hips and dried marigolds. The finished pot pourri is then decorated with peach roses and whole fruits studded with cloves.

Ingredients

Dried fruit and flowers (see above)

15g (½oz) of orris root powder

80-90 drops of essential oil (here, 60 drops sweet orange oil and 30 drops cinnamon; one teaspoon holds about 60 drops)

Ceramic or glass bowl for mixing

Metal spoon

1 Place all the fruit and flower ingredients into the bowl, except the special pieces intended for decoration. If you want to alter the colour or texture, now is the time to vary the ingredients or their quantities. Pine cones would go well with this mixture, as would other lumpy seed heads or even nuts.

2 Count the number of drops required into the bowl; stir gently, using a metal spoon, then add the powdered orris root and stir well, taking great care not to break up any of the ingredients. If you do not require such a long-lasting scent, the orris root can be omitted and the oil stirred into the mix alone. The scent will fade much more quickly, but you can re-oil the mixture, using the same technique, once the perfume is too faint.

3 Tip the mixture into a large polythene bag and tie firmly at the neck. Place in a warm, dark cupboard and leave for one to two weeks, shaking or stirring the bag regularly to distribute the fragrance and ingredients. This allows the scents to blend and mellow before you place the mixture on display. When it has had a chance to mature, place the pot pourri in a bowl to display it, decorating the top with clove-studded fruits and roses or any other ingredients of your choice.

Perfumed straw hat

A straw hat can be prettily decorated with preserved summer flowers and transformed into a beautiful creation that could either be enjoyed as an arrangement on the wall or worn on a special occasion. Add some perfume oil to give an extra dimension to this arrangement and to any baskets of dried flowers that you might have in the house, using either a pot pourri reviver oil or a pure essential oil. You will need the following dried materials: 10 'Gerdo' roses, which are a pinky peach, and 10 'Calypso', which are a golden-apricot shade; one bunch of gypsophila, which is off-white; one bunch of green wheat; one of green amaranthus, and 20 apricot helichrysum heads.

Ingredients

Flowers and grasses (see above)

One adult-sized straw hat, approximately 40cm (16in) across, including the brim

1m (3ft) each of two ribbons, both 5cm (2in) wide

A glue gun and glue

1 Hold the ribbons together, and fold them in a figure of eight (see page 48). Make a bow with long streamers. Make sure the loops are not too large or they will not sit well on the brim of the hat. Glue the bow firmly to the right-angle where the crown meets the brim.

2 Make the wheat into small bunches about 7.5cm (3in) long and wire them firmly. Glue these around the hat. Make the amaranthus into bunches of a similar size and add these to the wheat. Next, make the gypsophila into neat bunches, again about 5–7.5cm (2–3in) long, and attach these around the brim. Gypsophila air dries very successfully in about a week, either hanging or in a dry bucket.

3 Finally, add the flowers to your design. The roses make a greater impact arranged in groups of three rather than individually dotted around the hat. Likewise the helichrysums, particularly if they have fairly small heads, can be arranged in groups and placed among the wheat and amaranthus. If you are going to hang the hat up on a wall, hold it up at the correct angle several times to check the effect, rather than keeping it flat on the table the whole time you are adding flowers to the design.

Bath oil, cologne & Lavender-scented pomander

Making your own bath oil and cologne is amazingly simple and very satisfying. Display the resulting potions in pretty glass perfume bottles and they will look as wonderful as they smell. The lavender-scented pomander is made from a selection of flowers, but has some lavender oil to boost the natural fragrances.

Bath oil and cologne

Making your own cosmetics is one way to ensure that only the best ingredients are used! The bath oil is a simple mixture of almond oil and essential oil, in this case lavender. You can ring the changes by using a different essential oil; you might like to consult an aromatherapy book to find a suitable oil to treat fatigue or depression, to relax or stimulate, to help aches and pains or to concentrate the mind. The fragrance of the cologne is also provided by its essential oil, which can be altered to suit your mood. Lavender oil has many properties, and will help with aches and pains, depression, fatigue and stress-related headaches.

Ingredients

Lavender bath oil:
100ml (6tbsp) almond oil

15ml (1tbsp) pure lavender essential oil

Screw-top jar, for mixing

Lavender cologne:
250ml (7fl oz) distilled water

15ml (1tbsp) vodka

5ml (1tsp) pure lavender essential oil

Screw-top jar, for mixing

Lavender bath oil

1 For the bath oil, use a large screw-top jar and mix the almond oil with the lavender oil by screwing down the lid and shaking thoroughly. It is very important to use best quality lavender oil from a reliable source (see page 48).

2 Decant the oil into an attractive container with a tightly fitting lid. If the oil is a gift, add a ribbon bow, together with a gift tag and brief instructions (add one tablespoon to a bath under fast running water).

Lavender cologne

1 *Mix all the ingredients in a large screw-top jar and, with the lid firmly on, shake very vigorously for a minute or so. As for the bath oil, make sure you use the very best quality lavender oil for this cologne.*

2 *Decant the mixture into an attractive bottle, preferably with a ground glass stopper, and label with a ribboned gift tag. An old alternative recipe uses dry white wine (still, not sparkling) instead of the water and vodka; this produces a different but interesting result. This cologne can either be added to bathwater or applied neat to the skin; it feels wonderful in the heat of summer if it is kept in the refrigerator.*

Lavender-scented pomander

When space is at a premium and there is little room for dried flowers in baskets or as wall hanging displays, this hanging pomander could be ideal as a decoration. There is a little natural fragrance from the lavender used in making the pomander, but the scent has been enhanced by the addition of some lavender oil sprinkled onto the flowers after the pomander was finished. You will need a small bunch of sea lavender, which in this example has been dyed a pale lavender blue, one bunch of medium-sized poppy seed heads, one of echinops, one bunch of English or French lavender, a bunch of brunia (an exotic seed head), and 30 cream helichrysum heads.

Ingredients

Dried flowers and seed heads (see above)

Approximately 1m (3ft) of cord, for hanging (the length can be longer or shorter, as desired)

50cm (20in) of ribbon, 2.5cm (1in) wide, for bows at the top of the sphere

Dry foam sphere, 9cm (3½in) in diameter

0.71mm (22 gauge) florists' wires

1 Fold the cord in half and wind a wire firmly around the two cut ends, leaving a long leg. Push this through the foam ball, burying the cord ends. Trim the projecting wire to about 12mm–2.5cm (½–1in); bend it back on itself, and bury it in the foam. Make two bows from the ribbon (see page 48) and glue one to each side of the base of the loop.

2 Cover the ball with the sea lavender. Do not cover it too thickly or there will be no room for the other ingredients, but also beware using too little material and thus leaving gaps through which the foam will be visible. Next, start adding the poppy heads and echinops. They can either be pushed in at random or placed in groups, according to your taste. Use the smaller echinops in the bunch as some heads may be too large and would overshadow the other ingredients.

3 Place some of the brunia in the ball, dividing it into small clusters rather than trying to use whole stems. The helichrysum heads can be placed in next; you can either glue the heads in position or, as in this case, use wired helichrysums, which slide into the foam easily. Finally, divide the lavender into small bunches; wire each bunch firmly but gently, and distribute the bunches throughout the ball. If you want the ball to smell more strongly of lavender, drop some lavender essential oil onto the flowers and seed heads and leave it to soak in.

Fragrant flowers in terracotta

If you have scented flowers or plants in your garden you can arrange something lovely in the house very easily. Even if you have to add to the quantity with a few flowers bought from the florist this still makes an arrangement a relatively inexpensive way of giving yourself a great deal of pleasure.

Fragrant flowers in terracotta

A simple group of flowers arranged in a selection of containers can look strikingly effective, yet couldn't be simpler to arrange. The terracotta containers used here have been painted to tone with their surroundings. Here, I have used a medley of highly scented flowers – a bunch of lilies of the valley, some stephanotis, lilac and phlox.

Ingredients

Flowers (see above)

A selection of containers – here, two vases 20cm (8in) high, one bowl 17.5cm (7in) in diameter, a couple of small flowerpots 7.5cm (3in) in diameter

Six or seven small sea shells

1 Arrange the taller ingredients in the larger vases. Make sure they have plenty of water, and cut the stems on a slant to make sure that the stems do not touch the base of the container, preventing water from passing up the stalks.

2 Position a few shells on the base of the bowl and fill the bowl with water. Place the stephanotis in the water – some heads together and some individually. The individual heads will only float facing upwards if you shorten the length of the flower trumpet; without this, they will turn on their sides.

3 Seal the holes in the small flowerpots and stack them one inside another to give more height. Fill the top pot with water and place the bunch of lilies of the valley and some leaves inside the flowerpot. The mixed perfumes of these highly scented flowers are quite delicious!

Useful tips & Addresses

For dried flower and pot pourri courses:

Joanna Sheen Limited
P.O. Box 52
Newton Abbot
Devon TQ12 4QH

For dried flowers:
The Hop Shop
Castle Farm
Shoreham
Sevenoaks
Kent TN14 7UB

For lavender oil and other lavender products:
Jersey Lavender
Rue de Pont Marquet
St. Brelade
Jersey
Channel Islands

Norfolk Lavender
Caley Mill
Heacham
Kings Lynn
Norfolk PE31 7JE

Essential oils

Essential oils are distilled from fruit, leaves, flowers and bark and are very different to the mixed perfume oils and chemical fragrances that are sold as pot pourri reviver oils. The latter are perfectly acceptable for use in pot pourri work or for scenting dried flower arrangements, but I would recommend using essential oils in any skin preparations such as the lavender bath oil or cologne.

Suggested suppliers of essential oils:
Shirley Price
Wesley House
Stockwell Head
Hinkley
Leics. LE10 1RD

The Tisserand Institute
P.O. Box 746
Hove
East Sussex BN17 7LR

To make a bow, take a length of ribbon and fold it into loops, as shown. Bind the loops at one end with a stub wire, and use the ends of the wire to insert the bow into the arrangement.